GROSS STUFF IN YOUR BODY

BY PAM ROSENBERG

ILLUSTRATED BY BEATRIZ HELENA RAMOS

ABOUT THE AUTHOR:

Pam Rosenberg lives in Illinois with a husband, two kids, two cats, a hermit crab, a few bugs, and lots of bacteria and other tiny things she doesn't like to think about.

ABOUT THE ILLUSTRATOR:

Beatriz Helena Ramos is an artist from Venezuela who lives and plays in NYC. She works from her animation studio, Dancing Diablo, where she directs animated spots. Beatriz has illustrated a dozen books and she particularly loves gross stories.

The Child's World

Published by The Child's World®
1980 Lookout Drive • Mankato, MN 56003-1705
800-599-READ • www.childsworld.com

Photos: CSIRO, CC BY 3.0, via Wikimedia Commons: 19
Dimarion/Shutterstock.com: cover, 12; whitehoune/Shutterstock.com: 17

ISBN 9781503850194 (Reinforced Library Binding)
ISBN 9781503850682 (Portable Document Format)
ISBN 9781503851443 (Online Multi-user eBook)
LCCN: 2021930124

Printed in the United States of America

TABLE OF CONTENTS

EEW!

DID YOU EVER STOP TO THINK ABOUT ALL THE ICKY, STICKY, GROSS STUFF THAT'S PART OF YOU?

If you want to learn more, here's a head-to-toe look at the human body. Turn the page—if you dare!

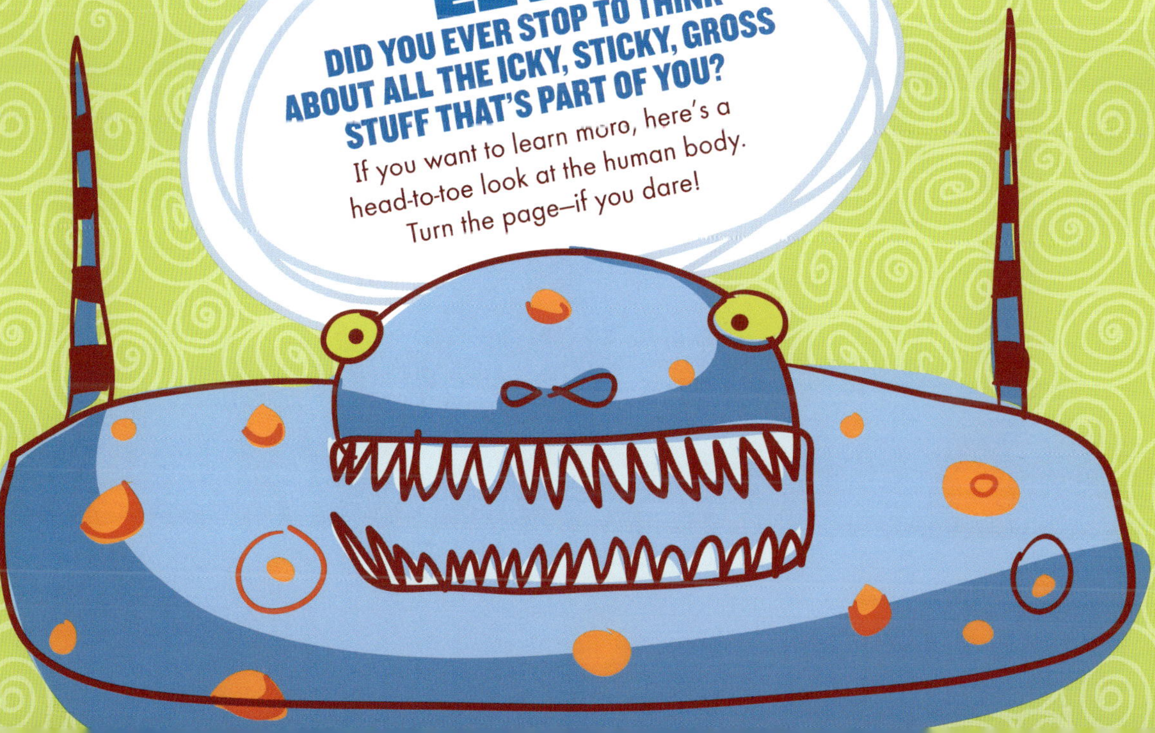

HAIR AND OTHER HEADY STUFF

What are those white flakes falling off your head and decorating your shoulders? They are dead skin cells mixed with oil from your scalp—otherwise known as **dandruff**.

What has six legs and no wings? It's a head louse. If a group of these sesame-seed sized bugs ends up on your head, you have one bad case of head lice! These bugs grab onto your scalp with their teeth and insert a sharp "straw" from their mouths. Then they suck your blood!

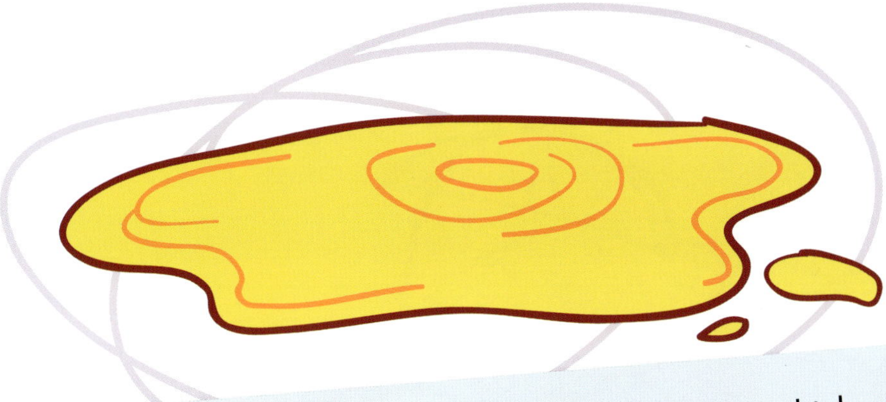

Tears are mostly water. There is a little **sodium** in them, which gives them that salty taste. But they also have stuff like ammonia, acid, and calcium. **Do you know what else in your body has lots of the same ingredients as tears?** If you said pee, give yourself an A+!

What's that goo in your nose? It's called **mucus**. Your body makes it to trap dirt and germs that make it up your nostrils and past your nose hairs. Your body makes about a quart of the stuff every day. If thinking about that isn't yucky enough, guess how much of the stuff you swallow every day? Two cups!

Scientists say that some sneezes travel at more than 100 miles per hour (161 kilometers per hour)! That might not sound too disgusting until you realize how many germs are in that spray from your nose. And some of those germs can hang around in the air for a long time—maybe even an hour!

Did you know that you have hair inside your ears? Yep, your inner ears have tiny hairs in them. These tiny hairs are attached to **nerves**. Sounds that enter your ear make the tiny hairs **vibrate**. Then the nerves send signals to your brain and you hear the sounds. If you had no hairs in your inner ears, no signals would reach your brain and you wouldn't be able to hear.

Did you ever smell your breath first thing in the morning? Well, your mom has, and it isn't pretty. Ever wonder why morning breath is so stinky? Your mouth is filled with spit. There are **chemicals** in spit that help kill bacteria. That's a good thing, because your mouth has about 10 billion **bacteria** in it! But at night your body doesn't make as much spit, so the bacteria have a chance to grow. That's what makes your mouth stink.

Want a secret weapon against bacteria and stinky breath? You already have one—your toothbrush. Use it every morning to do your part to save the world from smelly bacteria!

WHAT GOES IN MUST COME OUT

It isn't the food or the water heading down into your stomach that makes you burp. It's the air you swallow along with the food and water. And when that air decides to come back up, look out—**BUUURRPPPP!**

What happens in your stomach? Strong acids break all the food down into a soupy liquid. Why don't the acids eat up the inside of your stomach? Because your stomach is lined with mucus—the same slimy goo that lines the inside of your nose, mouth, and throat!

Food leaves your stomach and heads into your small intestine. An adult has about 20 feet (6 meters) of small intestines coiled up inside his or her body. That's where all of the **nutrients** are absorbed into your body. Whatever is left over heads to the next stop—the large intestine. That's where all of the extra water is taken out of the leftover bits of food and those leftovers officially become poop.

Did you know that there are lots of bacteria in your intestines? It helps break down your food. In the process it produces gas, sometimes lots of it. How does your body get rid of that gas? We pass gas—the average person passes gas about fourteen times a day!

Take a guess: How much do you think the average person eats in a day? If you said about 3 pounds (1.5 kilograms) of food, you are correct. If you live to be 70, you'll have eaten about 33 tons of the stuff.

How much of that becomes poop?

About enough to make a pile of poo the size of a car!

Did you know that you can stand on your head and eat?

Food would still get to your stomach because the muscles in your guts would still push it down there.

You probably know what happens if you eat too much. Your stomach has to get rid of that food somehow. So your **digestive system** goes into reverse. The muscles that were working to push the food down and into your intestines start pushing the food back up and out of your mouth until you vomit—puke—toss your cookies. But all that yucky stuff doesn't taste anything like cookies. That nasty taste in your mouth after puking comes from the acids in your stomach coming back up with the partially digested food. Quick, get some mouthwash!

Speaking of stuff that comes out of your body, did you know that you get rid of about 2 pints (1 liter) of pee a day?

Pee—also known as **urine**—is the extra water and tiny bits of waste that your kidneys filter out of your blood. Your kidneys work hard—they clean about 44 gallons (167 liters) of blood a day!

And speaking of blood . . .

VAMPIRES LOVE IT, YOU SHOULD TOO—BLOOD

A single drop of blood is made up of 250 thousand blood cells! In fact, your heart is pumping about 30 trillion of those little guys through your body right now.

Did you ever squash a mosquito on your arm and see blood? That was your blood, not the mosquito's! Female mosquitoes need the protein from blood to make baby mosquitoes. So they stick their **proboscis**, which is like a tiny straw, through your skin and drink your blood. Their saliva keeps your blood from clotting so they can get a nice long drink. Yum!

You probably know that human blood is red. But not all animals have red blood. Some ocean worms have green blood. Crabs have blue blood. Some animals even have clear blood!

Blood vessels called *arteries, veins,* and *capillaries* carry your blood throughout your body. Every human body has about 60,000 miles (96,500 kilometers) of blood vessels.

What do onions and garlic have to do with your blood? You might think that the bad breath you get from eating them comes from your mouth. But it really comes from your lungs. The stuff that causes onions and garlic to stink gets in your blood. When your blood circulates through your lungs, you breathe out the smelly gas!

GET MOVING!

There are more than 600 muscles in your body. They are made up of stretchy stuff, kind of like having a bunch of rubber bands in your body!

Some of your muscles are controlled by you. Those are the skeletal muscles. They take care of the kinds of movements that you can control—like walking, swinging a baseball bat, kicking a soccer ball, or writing with a pencil. Other muscles aren't controlled by you. They are the smooth muscles. They take care of things that happen whether you think about them or not. These include things like blinking and breathing.

Your heart is made up of a special kind of muscle called cardiac muscle. It pumps and forces your blood to move throughout your body. The average person's heart will beat about 3 billion times in a lifetime.

Your eye muscles do a lot of work. Besides holding your eyeballs in your head, they move them around. They probably move about 100,000 times a day!

Where is the largest muscle in your body? In your butt! It's called the *gluteus maximus* (GLOO-tee-yuss MAX-ih-muss).

Did you know that your tongue is made up of muscles? Its muscles help you chew and swallow your food and help you make certain sounds. The tongue is attached to the bottom of your mouth. So go ahead and try, but you just can't swallow your tongue!

YOU'VE GOT A LOT OF NERVE

Without your brain, none of your muscles would work. But your brain isn't a muscle. It's a big blob of spongy-yet-solid gray stuff in your head. It's kind of like a big, gray cauliflower made of hardened **gelatin**.

That big cauliflower—otherwise known as your brain—sends signals to your muscles to make them do the things you want them to do. It also sends the signals to your body to make it do the things you need it to do so you stay alive—like breathing!

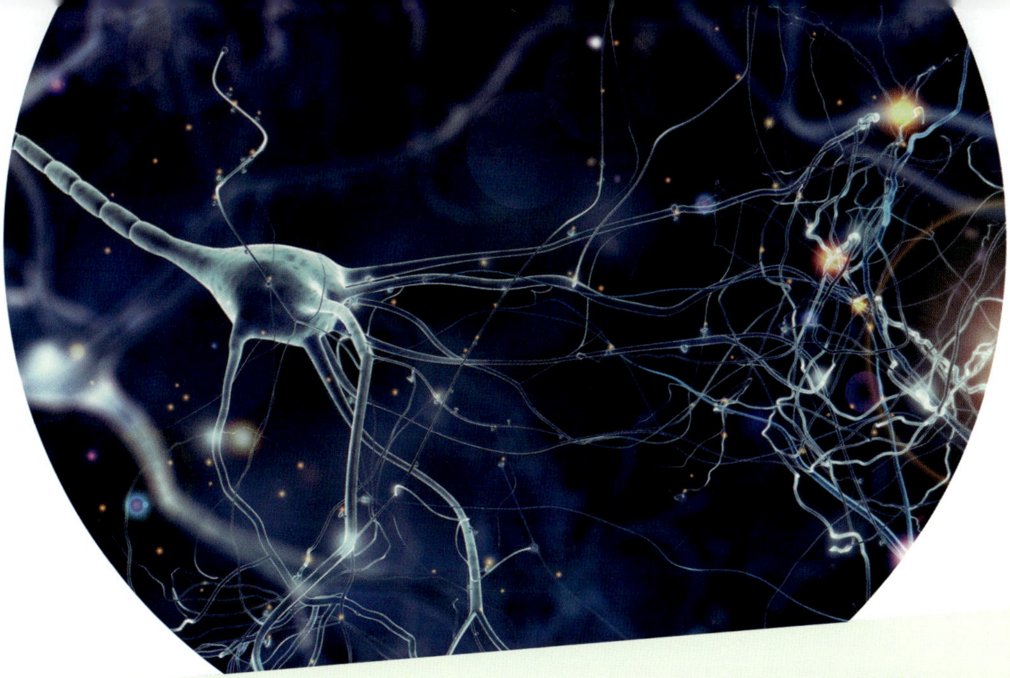

Your brain is made up of about 100 billion nerve cells, called neurons. There are nerve cells throughout your body, and they are all connected to each other and to your brain. Let's say you touch a hot stove. You feel pain right away and you move your hand away. That's because the signal from your hand was sent along this nerve pathway to your brain and back at a speed of 350 feet (107 meters) per second!

Signals from your brain let you know when some part of your body hurts, but your brain doesn't feel pain. That's right, you could slice right into your brain and you wouldn't feel a thing!

THE SKIN YOU'RE IN

Skin is the largest organ of your body. It is waterproof and stretchy. It keeps your insides in and germs and dirt out.

Lots of bacteria and viruses can cause skin rashes. Did you ever have chicken pox? It starts out as small, red bumps that look like pimples. Then they turn into blisters filled with a clear liquid. Then the blister breaks and you have open sores. They crust over and form dry, brown scabs. Oh, and they itch. A lot!

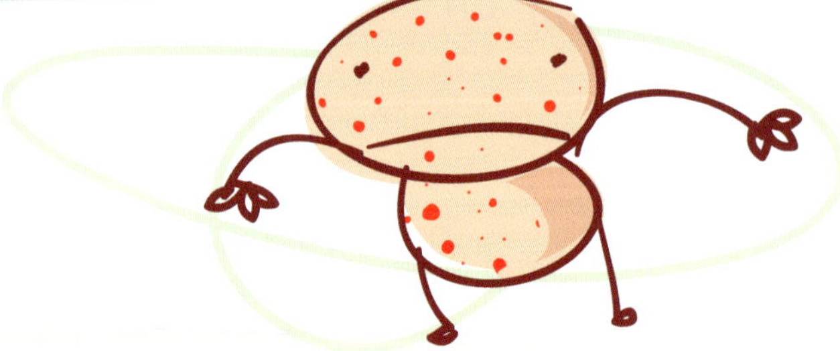

Some kinds of plants can make your skin itch, too. The oil in the poison ivy plant that causes the itchy rash you get if you touch it is called **urushiol**. This stuff is so strong that an amount the size of the head of a pin could make 500 people itchy!

About 30,000 to 40,000 dead skin cells fall off your body every minute. In your lifetime, you'll shed about 40 pounds (18 kilograms) of skin. Think that's gross? You're house is filled with teeny, tiny bugs that you can't see, called dust mites. Your dead skin cells are their favorite food. Next time you crawl into your nice warm bed, try not thinking about all of the little bugs hanging out in your mattress waiting for their next meal to arrive–you!

The skin you and your family and friends shed makes up about 70 percent of the dust in your house. Maybe we should call those hungry, invisible bugs "skin mites"!

If you took all of the skin off an adult and laid it out flat, you'd have a skin sheet large enough to cover a queen-sized bed!

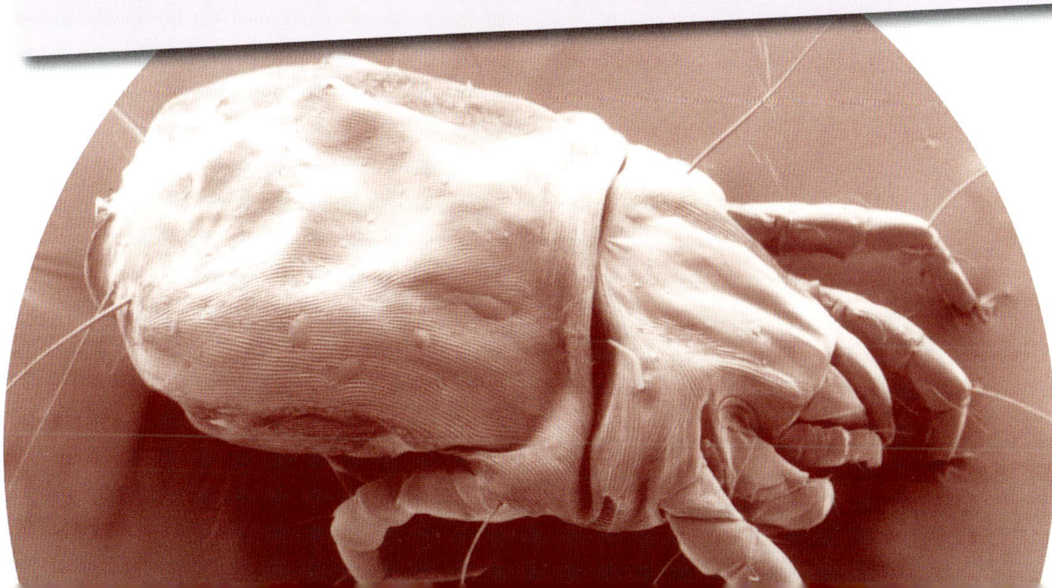

TRICK OR TREAT, SMELL MY FEET!

Each of your feet has twenty-six bones in it. So, together your feet have about 1/4 of the bones in your body!

You may want to remember how many bones are in your feet if you ever wear shoes that are too tight. If you do that for a long time, especially if your big toe is the one getting squished, the bones in your toes will rebel. You'll end up with a **bunion**—a big ugly bone bump that sticks out on the side of your foot. Oh, and did I forget to mention that a bunion really, really hurts?

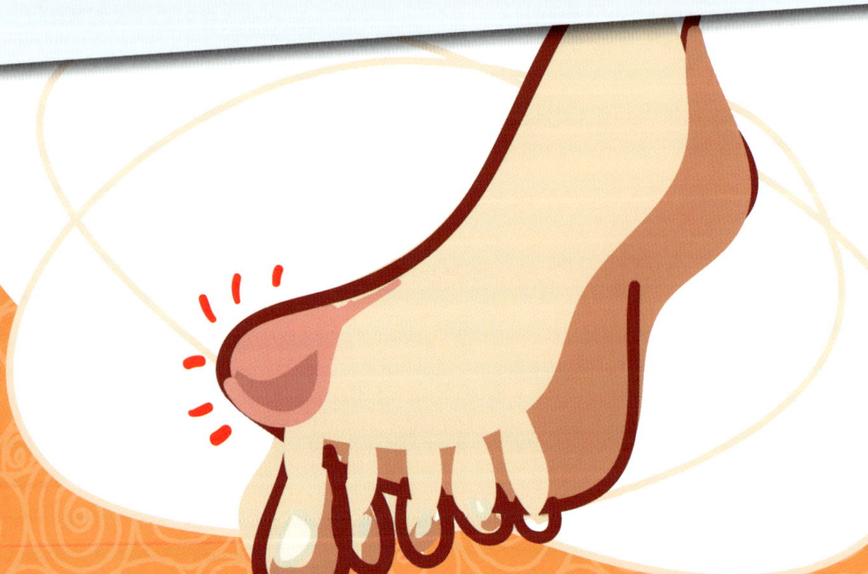

Did you know that your feet contain about 250,000 sweat glands? That means your feet can make about 1 cup (237 milliliters) of sweat a day!

All of that nice, warm sweat helps make your feet the preferred home of ringworm. No, it's not really a worm, it's a kind of **fungus**—a living thing that takes root in the upper layers of your skin. It feeds on the protein that makes up part of your skin. And you end up with cracked, red, itchy, nasty-looking skin on your feet.

You probably know that viruses cause colds and flu, but did you know that they cause warts too? Plantar warts grow on your feet. So if you see something kind of spongy and gray or brown growing on the bottom of your feet, go see a doctor!

So, if you want to know more about your body, use your feet to head over to your local library. The trip will be just a small part of the nearly 115,000 miles (185,075 kilometers) it's estimated the average human will walk in a lifetime. That's enough walking to circle Earth four times!

GLOSSARY

bacteria (bak-TEER-ee-uh) Bacteria are microscopic living things. The spit in your mouth helps to kill bacteria.

blood vessels (BLUHD VES-uhl) Blood vessels are thin tubes that carry blood through your body. Arteries, veins, and capillaries are kinds of blood vessels.

bunion (BUN-yuhn) A bunion is a swelling of the big toe that causes the joint to stick out and become painful. If you wear shoes that are too tight, you can develop a bunion.

cardiac (KAR-dee-ak) Cardiac describes something that is related to the heart. Your heart is made up of a special kind of muscle called cardiac muscle.

chemicals (KEM-uh-kuhlz) Chemicals are substances that are used in chemistry, the study of what substances are made of and how they react with one another. There are chemicals in human spit that help kill bacteria.

dandruff (DAN-druff) Dandruff is small white flakes of dead skin from your scalp. Dandruff often falls off your head and ends up on your shoulders.

digestive system (dy-JEST-iv SIS-tuhm) The digestive system is made up of all of the organs that help to break down the food that you eat so it can be absorbed into your bloodstream and used by your body. When you vomit, your digestive system starts working in reverse and pushes partially digested food back up through your mouth.

fungus (FUN-guss) A fungus is a living organism that reproduces by creating spores. Ringworm is a kind of fungus that lives on your skin.

gelatin (JEL-uh-tin) Gelatin is a clear substance that comes from bones and other animal parts and is used in making jelly and some desserts. The human brain looks a little like a gray cauliflower made of gelatin.

glands (GLANDZ) Glands are organs in the body that produce chemicals or help chemicals leave the body. Your feet have about 250,000 sweat glands in them.

mucus (MYOO-kuss) Mucus is the sticky liquid that lines the inside of your nose, throat, mouth and some other body parts. Mucus helps trap dirt and germs that get into your nose.

nerves (NURVZ) Nerves are the thin fibers that send messages between your brain and spinal cord and other parts of your body. Nerves attached to tiny hairs in your ears send signals to your brain so you can hear sounds.

neurons (NOOR-onz) Neurons are individual nerve cells. Your brain is made up of about 100 billion neurons.

nutrients (NOO-tree-uhnts) Nutrients are things that supply nourishment to your body. Nutrients are absorbed into your body as they travel through the small intestine.

proboscis (pruh-BAH-siss) A proboscis is a long flexible tube used by an insect to take in fluids. A female mosquito sticks her sharp proboscis into your skin to drink your blood.

sodium (SOH-dee-uhm) Sodium is a chemical found in salt. The sodium in human tears makes them taste salty.

urine (YUR-en) Urine is the liquid waste that humans and animals pass out of their bodies. Urine is the extra water and bits of waste that is filtered out of your blood by your kidneys.

urushiol (yur-OO-shee-all) Urushiol is an oil found in poison ivy plants. Urushiol is the substance that causes people to develop an itchy rash when they touch a poison ivy plant.

vibrate (VY-brayt) To vibrate means to move back and forth quickly. Sounds that enter your ears make the tiny hairs inside your ears vibrate.

viruses (VY-ruhss-ez) Viruses are living things that are smaller than bacteria and cause diseases. The itchy rash of chicken pox is caused by a virus.

FOR MORE INFORMATION

Cole, Joanna. *The Magic School Bus: Inside the Human Body.* New York, NY: Scholastic, 1989.

DK and The Smithsonian Institution. *Human Body!* New York, NY: Smithsonian, 2017.

Wilsdon, Christina. *Ultimate Bodypedia: An Amazing Inside-Out Tour of the Human Body.* Washington, DC: National Geographic 2014.

Visit our website to learn more about gross stuff in your body:
childsworld.com/links

Note to Parents, Teachers, and Librarians: We routinely verify our weblinks to make sure they are safe, active sites—so encourage your readers to check them out!

INDEX